I0704780
MAKE POLITICS AGAIN!
MAKE POLITICS
MAKE POLITIC FUN
MAKE POLITICS FUN AGAIN
EXPLORING
THE TRUTH BEHIND
THE MAGA MOVEMENT
MAKE POLITICS FUN AGAIN
MAGA and MAHA
MIKE MARKUSON

Disclaimer

The content in this ebook, Make Politics Fun Again: Exploring the Truth Behind the MAGA Movement, was generated with the help of an artificial intelligence. While we aim to sprinkle a bit of humor into the often serious world of politics, we are not political analysts, comedians, or fortune tellers (despite what our algorithms might suggest).

This ebook is intended for educational and entertainment purposes only. Before you take any political advice or start a debate with your Uncle Bob at Thanksgiving, please consult with real experts or at least Google the topic!

We can't guarantee that your political views will change, that you'll find common ground, or that you won't accidentally start an internet argument. Just remember: laughter is the best politics!

In short: Don't just take our word for it—trust the professionals... or at least your favorite late-night talk show host!

"Still it is good info and I recommend it!"

–   Mike

Table of Contents

Make Politics Fun Again: Exploring the Truth Behind the MAGA Movement

Chapter 1: The Rise of the MAGA Movement

The Rise of the MAGA Movement

The Make America Great Again (MAGA) movement burst onto the political scene in 2015, when then-businessman Donald Trump announced his candidacy for President. With his campaign slogan emblazoned on red hats across the country, Trump tapped into a sentiment shared by many Americans who felt disillusioned with the political establishment and yearned for change.

But where did the idea of making America great again come from? The phrase itself has a long history in American politics, dating back to Ronald Reagan's 1980 presidential campaign. Reagan's promise to restore American greatness struck a chord with voters weary of economic turmoil and international challenges.

Fast forward to 2015, and Trump's use of the slogan breathed new life into the concept of American greatness. His supporters, known as Trumpsters, were drawn to his unapologetic stance on issues like immigration, trade, and national security. They saw him as a political outsider who could shake up Washington and bring about the change they craved.

As Trump's campaign gained traction, the MAGA movement evolved from a catchy slogan to a full-fledged political phenomenon. Supporters attended rallies in droves, chanting "Build the Wall" and "Lock Her Up" with fervor. The movement became synonymous with populism, nationalism, and a rejection of political correctness.

The impact of the MAGA movement on American politics cannot be overstated. Trump's victory in the 2016 election sent shockwaves through the establishment, proving that a brash businessman from

Queens could defy the odds and win the highest office in the land. His presidency ushered in a new era of political polarization, with supporters and opponents alike fiercely divided over his policies and rhetoric.

As the first half of this chapter comes to a close, it's clear that the MAGA movement has left an indelible mark on American politics. But how did it shape the landscape for years to come? What were the key moments that defined its rise to power? Stay tuned for the second half of our exploration into the truth behind the MAGA movement. The Rise of the MAGA Movement

As the Make America Great Again (MAGA) movement continued to gain momentum, it became clear that Donald Trump had tapped into something powerful in the American psyche. His bold rhetoric and unorthodox approach to politics resonated with millions of voters who were tired of the status quo and hungry for change.

One of the key factors that fueled the rise of the MAGA movement was Trump's skillful use of social media. Throughout his campaign and presidency, he leveraged platforms like Twitter to communicate directly with his supporters and bypass traditional media channels. His controversial tweets sparked debates, drove news cycles, and solidified his image as a political disruptor.

Trump's ability to connect with his base on a personal level was another crucial element in the success of the MAGA movement. His "America First" message struck a chord with working-class voters who felt left behind by globalism and elite interests. By promising to bring back jobs, secure the border, and protect American interests, Trump tapped into a sense of national pride and identity that resonated with many.

The MAGA movement also drew strength from its fervent supporters, who were passionate, vocal, and unapologetic in their defense of Trump and his policies. They attended rallies in droves, proudly wearing their red MAGA hats and chanting slogans that became rallying cries for the movement. Trump's ability to galvanize his base and turn their energy into political action was a defining feature of his presidency.

But as the MAGA movement rose in popularity, it also faced fierce opposition from critics who viewed Trump's rhetoric as divisive, inflammatory, and dangerous. The polarization and vitriol that characterized American politics during Trump's tenure were unlike anything the country had seen in recent memory. Supporters and opponents alike clashed in the streets, on social media, and in the halls of government, leading to a level of acrimony and hostility that threatened to tear the fabric of society apart.

Despite the controversies and challenges that confronted the MAGA movement, it continued to wield significant influence in American politics. Trump's presidency marked a turning point in the country's political landscape, ushering in an era of populism, nationalism, and confrontation. The legacy of the MAGA movement would endure long after Trump left office, shaping debates, policies, and elections for years to come.

As we reflect on the rise of the MAGA movement, it is clear that its impact on American politics was profound and far-reaching. It challenged conventions, galvanized supporters, and transformed the way we think about leadership and governance. The truth behind the MAGA movement is a complex and multifaceted story, full of highs and lows, triumphs and setbacks. And as we look to the future, it remains to be seen how the legacy of the MAGA movement will continue to shape the course of American history.

POLITICAL
DEBATE

Chapter 2: Understanding Political Polarization

Political polarization in the United States has reached new heights in recent years, with Republicans and Democrats becoming more divided than ever. The question on everyone's minds is: why has this divide grown so wide?

One of the main reasons behind this growing political polarization is the rise of identity politics. In today's society, individuals often align themselves with a certain political party based on their personal identity, rather than their beliefs on actual policy issues. This has led to increased tribalism within the political sphere, as people are more likely to support their party at all costs, rather than engage in meaningful dialogue with those who hold different views.

Another factor contributing to political polarization is the influence of social media and the echo chambers it creates. People are now able to curate their online experiences to only see information that reinforces their own beliefs, leading to a lack of exposure to diverse perspectives. This further entrenches individuals in their own ideologies, making it challenging to find common ground with those who hold opposing views.

Additionally, the media landscape has played a significant role in fueling political polarization. With the rise of 24-hour news networks and opinion-driven journalism, viewers are often exposed to biased reporting that reinforces their preconceived notions. This has led to a lack of trust in the media on both sides of the political spectrum, further deepening the divide between Republicans and Democrats.

The political polarization in the United States is also exacerbated by the increasing influence of money in politics. Special interest groups and wealthy donors often have significant influence over politicians, leading to policy decisions that may not always align with the best interests of the general population. This perceived corruption within the political system has only served to widen the gap between Republicans and Democrats, as trust in government institutions continues to erode.

As we continue to delve into the reasons behind the growing divide between Republicans and Democrats, it becomes apparent that there are a multitude of factors at play. From identity politics to social media echo chambers, the landscape of American politics is more polarized than ever before. In the next part of this chapter, we will explore potential solutions to bridge this gap and foster a more united political climate. Stay tuned for more insights on understanding political polarization. Now that we've uncovered some of the reasons behind the political polarization in the United States, let's explore potential solutions to bridge this gap and foster a more united political climate. It's time to make politics fun again and find common ground among all Americans, regardless of their political affiliations.

One of the key solutions to combat political polarization is to prioritize civil discourse and respectful communication. Instead of resorting to personal attacks or aggressive arguments, it is important to engage in constructive conversations with those who hold different viewpoints. By listening actively, seeking to understand the perspectives of others, and finding areas of agreement, we can break down the walls of polarization and build bridges of understanding.

Furthermore, promoting media literacy and critical thinking skills can help combat the influence of biased reporting and misinformation that exacerbate political polarization. Encouraging individuals to fact-check information, seek out diverse sources, and think critically about the information they consume can help to combat the spread of fake news and promote a more informed electorate.

In addition, promoting policies that prioritize the interests of the general population over special interests and wealthy donors can help restore trust in government institutions and mitigate the perception of corruption in politics. By holding politicians accountable for their actions and advocating for transparency and integrity in the political process, we can work towards a more inclusive and equitable political system.

Another important step in bridging the political divide is to actively engage in community building and grassroots organizing. By coming together with fellow citizens to work towards common goals, we can create a sense of unity and purpose that transcends political differences. Whether it's volunteering for a local charity, participating in a community clean-up, or organizing a town hall meeting, taking tangible actions to improve our communities can help to foster a sense of shared humanity and common purpose.

Ultimately, breaking down political polarization requires a collective effort from all members of society. By prioritizing civil discourse, promoting media literacy, advocating for policies that prioritize the common good, and engaging in community building activities, we can work towards a more united and inclusive political climate.

As we continue to navigate the complex landscape of American politics, let us remember that we are all in this together. By seeking to understand each other, finding common ground, and working towards a shared vision of a better future, we can make politics fun again and build a more united and inclusive society for all. Together, we can bridge the political divide and create a more harmonious and peaceful future for generations to come.

VOTE
VOTE
VOTE
VOTE
VOTE FUN!
VOTE
VOTE

Chapter 3: The Art of Political Campaigning

Political campaigning is an art form with politicians using various strategies and tactics to attract voters and win elections. In order to be successful, politicians must carefully craft their image, message, and approach to appeal to their target audience.

One of the key strategies used by politicians is to establish a strong presence in the community through campaign events and outreach efforts. By attending local events, town hall meetings, and fundraisers, candidates can interact with voters on a personal level and gain their support. These interactions allow politicians to listen to voters' concerns, answer their questions, and show that they care about the issues that matter to them.

Another important tactic used by politicians is to develop a strong message that resonates with voters. This message should be clear, concise, and memorable, highlighting the candidate's key beliefs, values, and priorities. By crafting a compelling message, politicians can differentiate themselves from their competitors and rally supporters around their campaign.

In addition to their message, politicians must also carefully choose their campaign slogans, logos, and branding. These visual elements play a crucial role in shaping voters' perceptions of the candidate and their campaign. A catchy slogan, eye-catching logo, and cohesive branding can help politicians stand out in a crowded field and leave a lasting impression on voters.

Furthermore, politicians must be strategic in their use of media to communicate with voters. Whether through television ads, social media posts, or campaign websites, politicians must leverage various platforms to reach a wide audience and make their case to voters. By effectively utilizing media, politicians can amplify their message, target specific demographics, and engage voters in meaningful conversations about the issues that matter most.

Lastly, politicians must build a strong grassroots network of volunteers and supporters to help them reach voters and win elections. By organizing door-to-door canvassing, phone banking, and voter registration drives, politicians can mobilize their base, increase voter turnout, and maximize their chances of success on election day.

In conclusion, political campaigning is a complex and multifaceted process that requires careful planning, strategic thinking, and strong communication skills. By understanding the strategies and tactics used by politicians to attract voters and win elections, individuals can gain insight into the inner workings of the political process and the art of campaigning. Stay tuned for the second half of this chapter, where we will delve deeper into the world of political campaigning and explore additional techniques used by politicians to succeed in the world of politics.Now that we've covered the basics of political campaigning, let's dive deeper into some additional techniques used by politicians to succeed in the world of politics. One key element of a successful campaign is the use of endorsements from influential individuals and organizations. Endorsements can help build credibility, attract media attention, and sway undecided voters. Politicians often seek endorsements from celebrities, community leaders, unions, and advocacy groups to lend their support and boost their campaign.

Another important aspect of political campaigning is fundraising. Running for office requires a significant amount of money to pay for campaign staff, advertising, travel, and events. Politicians must actively fundraise by soliciting donations from individual donors, hosting fundraising events, and securing contributions from political action committees. By building a strong financial war chest, politicians can effectively compete in the electoral arena and reach a wider audience with their message.

In addition to endorsements and fundraising, politicians must also engage in debates and public speaking events to showcase their knowledge, skills, and vision for the future. Debates provide an opportunity for candidates to articulate their positions on key issues, defend their policies, and challenge their opponents. Public speaking events allow politicians to connect with voters, inspire change, and rally support for their campaign. By honing their public speaking skills, politicians can effectively communicate their message and earn the trust and confidence of the electorate.

Furthermore, politicians must be prepared to handle crisis communication and negative attacks from opponents. In today's fast-paced media landscape, scandals, controversies, and smear campaigns can quickly derail a candidate's chances of winning an election. Politicians must have a crisis communication plan in place to address negative publicity, respond to attacks, and protect their reputation. By staying composed, transparent, and focused on the issues that matter most to voters, politicians can weather the storm and emerge stronger on the other side.

Lastly, successful political campaigning requires a strong ground game and effective get-out-the-vote efforts. On election day, voter turnout can make or break a candidate's chances of victory. Politicians must mobilize their supporters, remind them to vote, and provide transportation to the polls if needed. By running a well-organized ground operation, politicians can maximize voter turnout, secure last-minute support, and edge out their opponents in a close race.

In conclusion, the art of political campaigning is a dynamic and ever-evolving process that requires creativity, determination, and strategic thinking. By mastering the strategies and tactics outlined in this chapter, aspiring politicians can navigate the complexities of the electoral landscape, connect with voters on a personal level, and ultimately achieve success in the world of politics. So remember, whether you're running for class president or aiming for higher office, the key to making politics fun again lies in understanding the art of political campaigning and using it to your advantage. Stay tuned for more insights and tips on how to engage, inspire, and lead in the exciting world of politics.

TRUTH
MATERS
Charged With
Spreading Fake News

Chapter 4: Fact vs Fiction in Political Discourse

False information and fake news have become pervasive in today's political discourse, shaping public opinion and influencing political decisions. With the rise of social media and the internet, misinformation spreads like wildfire, often blurring the lines between fact and fiction.

In the realm of politics, misinformation can be used as a tool to manipulate public perceptions and sow discord among the masses. Whether it's a misleading headline, a doctored image, or a fabricated quote, false information can easily go viral and have a lasting impact on people's beliefs and behaviors.

One of the biggest challenges in combating fake news is the sheer volume of information available online. With so much content being shared across various platforms, it can be difficult to discern what is true and what is false. This is where critical thinking skills come into play. It's important for individuals to question the source of the information, check for corroborating evidence, and be wary of sensationalized or biased content.

Unfortunately, not everyone takes the time to verify the accuracy of the information they encounter. This can lead to the spread of false narratives and the perpetuation of harmful stereotypes. In the political arena, misinformation can be used to demonize opponents, incite fear and distrust, and ultimately undermine the democratic process.

To make matters worse, some individuals and organizations actively work to spread misinformation for their own gain. Whether it's for financial profit, political advantage, or simply to cause chaos, these actors prey on people's emotions and vulnerabilities in order to advance their own agendas.

In the age of social media, it's more important than ever for individuals to be vigilant about the information they consume and share. By being mindful of the sources of information, fact-checking claims, and engaging critically with the content they encounter, people can help combat the spread of misinformation and fake news.

Ultimately, the battle against misinformation requires a collective effort from individuals, media outlets, and tech companies. It's crucial for everyone to prioritize truth and accuracy in political discourse, in order to uphold the integrity of our democratic institutions and ensure that informed decisions are made for the betterment of society.Now that we have explored the impact of misinformation and fake news in political discourse, let's delve into some practical steps that can be taken to combat the spread of false information and promote a more informed and accurate conversation.

First and foremost, it's important to educate ourselves and others on how to spot fake news. Encouraging critical thinking skills and media literacy can help individuals become more discerning consumers of information. By teaching people to question the source, evaluate the evidence, and consider alternative perspectives, we can empower them to navigate the complex landscape of online information with greater confidence.

Fact-checking websites can also be valuable tools in the fight against misinformation. Websites such as Snopes, FactCheck.org, and PolitiFact provide independent assessments of the accuracy of news stories, viral claims, and political statements. By consulting these sources, individuals can verify the credibility of information and avoid falling prey to false narratives.

Furthermore, building a diverse media diet can help to combat echo chambers and filter bubbles, which can contribute to the spread of misinformation. By seeking out news sources with different perspectives and political leanings, individuals can gain a more nuanced understanding of complex issues and avoid being trapped in a cycle of confirmation bias.

Engaging in civil discourse and respectful debate is also key to combating misinformation. By listening to opposing viewpoints, seeking common ground, and focusing on facts rather than emotions, we can foster a more constructive and honest dialogue. It's important to remember that everyone is entitled to their own opinions, but not their own facts.

Lastly, holding individuals and institutions accountable for spreading misinformation is crucial. Social media platforms, news outlets, and public figures should be held to high standards of accuracy and transparency. By calling out false information when we see it, we can help to create a culture of accountability and integrity in political discourse.

In conclusion, the battle against misinformation in politics is an ongoing challenge that requires vigilance, critical thinking, and a commitment to truth. By taking proactive steps to combat fake news, educate ourselves and others, and promote a more informed and respectful conversation, we can help to ensure that our democratic institutions remain strong and that informed decisions are made for the betterment of society.

So let's arm ourselves with knowledge, sharpen our critical thinking skills, and be the champions of truth in the political arena. Together, we can make politics fun again by upholding the principles of honesty, integrity, and accuracy in all our discussions and debates.

Debate has
gone Viral

Chapter 5: The Power of Social Media in Politics

Social media has become an integral part of modern politics, revolutionizing the way politicians communicate with the public. Platforms like Twitter and Facebook have given politicians a direct line of communication to their constituents, allowing them to bypass traditional media outlets and speak directly to their followers.

One of the key benefits of social media in politics is the ability to reach a wider audience in real-time. Politicians can now share their thoughts, opinions, and policy proposals with millions of people at the click of a button. This has opened up new opportunities for engagement and transparency, allowing voters to get a glimpse into the daily lives of their elected officials.

Twitter, in particular, has become a popular platform for politicians to communicate with the public. With its character limit, politicians are forced to distill their messages down to the most essential points, making it a quick and efficient way to share information. From announcing new policies to responding to political opponents, Twitter has become a powerful tool for politicians to shape public opinion.

Facebook, on the other hand, allows politicians to connect with their constituents on a more personal level. By sharing behind-the-scenes photos, hosting live Q&A sessions, and posting updates on their daily activities, politicians can create a sense of intimacy and authenticity with their followers. This humanizes politicians and makes them more relatable to the general public.

However, social media also comes with its challenges in the political sphere. The instant nature of these platforms can lead to hasty decisions and impulsive responses, which can have unintended consequences. Politicians must be careful about what they post online, as one wrong tweet or Facebook post can quickly spiral out of control and damage their reputation.

Furthermore, social media has also been criticized for creating echo chambers, where individuals only engage with like-minded people and are shielded from opposing viewpoints. This can lead to polarization and division, making it harder for politicians to find common ground and work together on bipartisan issues.

Despite these challenges, there is no denying the power of social media in shaping the political landscape. As we move forward, it will be crucial for politicians to strike a balance between utilizing social media to engage with the public while also upholding the values of transparency, authenticity, and accountability. By harnessing the full potential of platforms like Twitter and Facebook, politicians can truly make politics fun again and foster a more informed and engaged electorate. Now that we've explored the positives and negatives of social media in politics, let's delve deeper into how these platforms have influenced political movements and campaigns.

One of the most notable examples of social media's impact on politics is the rise of the MAGA movement. The Make America Great Again movement, spearheaded by former President Donald Trump, utilized platforms like Twitter and Facebook to connect with supporters, spread his message, and rally his base. Trump's use of social media was often controversial, with his tweets and posts sparking debates, outrage, and adoration from millions of followers. Whether you agree with his policies or not, there's no denying the power of social media in helping him connect with a wide audience and shape public opinion.

But the MAGA movement wasn't just about one man. It was a collective effort from supporters who used social media to organize rallies, share news articles, and engage in political discourse. Hashtags like #MAGA and #Trump2020 became rallying cries for those who believed in the movement's message of putting America first and making the country great again. Through social media, supporters were able to connect with like-minded individuals, share their views, and mobilize for political action.

Social media has also been instrumental in shaping broader political movements, such as the Black Lives Matter movement and the #MeToo movement. These grassroots campaigns have used platforms like Twitter and Facebook to raise awareness about social justice issues, mobilize supporters, and hold politicians and organizations accountable. By sharing personal stories, news articles, and organizing events, these movements have been able to make meaningful changes in society and push for social justice reform.

In addition to movements, social media has also played a key role in political campaigns. Candidates running for office use platforms like Twitter and Facebook to reach voters, fundraise, and share their policy platforms. The 2020 presidential election, for example, saw candidates from both parties using social media to connect with voters and promote their agendas. From live-streaming town halls to posting behind-the-scenes photos, politicians have leveraged social media to engage with the electorate in new and innovative ways.

As we look towards the future of politics and social media, it's important to recognize the power and influence these platforms have on shaping public opinion and driving political discourse. While there are challenges and pitfalls to navigate, the potential for engagement, transparency, and connection is vast. By harnessing the power of platforms like Twitter and Facebook, politicians can continue to make politics fun again and create a more informed and engaged electorate.

So next time you scroll through your social media feed, remember the impact these platforms have on shaping the political landscape. Whether you're a supporter, a critic, or somewhere in between, there's no denying the power of social media in making politics more accessible, engaging, and yes, even fun.

MAGA
MAGA
MAGA
MAGA
MAGA
MAGA
MAGA
MAGA
MAC
WOFEN

Chapter 6: The Impact of the MAGA Movement on Minority Communities

The Impact of the MAGA Movement on Minority Communities

As we delve into the realm of politics and examine the influence of the Make America Great Again movement on minority communities in the United States, it is crucial to take a closer look at the intricate dynamics at play. While the MAGA movement may have sparked a wave of support among certain segments of the population, its impact on minority groups has been a topic of intense debate and scrutiny.

One of the key areas where the MAGA movement has made a significant impact is in the realm of immigration policy. With the push for stricter border control and the infamous promise of building a wall along the southern border, the voices of immigrants and minority communities have been amplified in response to these divisive policies. The fear of deportation and family separation has created a sense of unease and uncertainty among immigrant communities, leading to heightened tensions and a sense of insecurity.

Furthermore, the rhetoric and messaging of the MAGA movement have often been perceived as divisive and exclusionary, particularly when it comes to issues of race and ethnicity. The emphasis on "America First" and the nostalgic call to "Make America Great Again" has raised concerns among minority communities about their place and status in a country that prides itself on diversity and inclusivity. The rise of nationalist sentiments and the resurgence of white supremacist ideologies have further exacerbated these concerns, leading to a sense of alienation and marginalization among minority groups.

In addition, the economic impact of the MAGA movement on minority communities cannot be overlooked. While the promise of revitalizing American industries and bringing back jobs to the heartland may have resonated with certain segments of the population, the reality has been far more complex. Minority communities, particularly those in urban centers and inner cities, have often been left behind in the wake of economic policies that prioritize certain industries and sectors over others. The widening wealth gap and the persistence of systemic inequalities have made it challenging for minority communities to thrive and prosper in the current political climate.

Overall, the influence of the MAGA movement on minority communities in the United States is a multifaceted and nuanced issue that warrants further exploration and analysis. As we continue to navigate the ever-changing landscape of American politics, it is essential to consider the voices and perspectives of all communities, regardless of race, ethnicity, or background. Only by engaging in constructive dialogue and fostering understanding can we truly make politics fun again. The impact of the MAGA movement on minority communities extends beyond just policies and rhetoric. It has also had a significant influence on the social and cultural fabric of America. The rise of nationalism and the resurgence of white supremacist ideologies have created a sense of division and polarization within society, leading to increased tensions and conflicts among different racial and ethnic groups.

One of the most notable consequences of the MAGA movement on minority communities is the rise in hate crimes and discrimination. Reports of racially motivated attacks and incidents have been on the rise since the inauguration of President Trump, with many minority groups feeling increasingly vulnerable and targeted. The normalization of xenophobic and racist language in political discourse has emboldened individuals with prejudiced beliefs to act out against minority communities, further perpetuating a cycle of fear and distrust.

Moreover, the impact of the MAGA movement on minority communities can also be seen in the realm of education and social mobility. The push for policies that prioritize certain industries and sectors over others has limited opportunities for economic advancement for many minority groups, especially those living in disadvantaged areas. The lack of investment in education and job training programs has further exacerbated the disparities in wealth and opportunity, making it difficult for minority communities to break the cycle of poverty and achieve upward social mobility.

Despite these challenges, minority communities have also shown resilience and strength in the face of adversity. Grassroots movements and community organizations have emerged to provide support and resources to those in need, fostering a sense of solidarity and empowerment among minority groups. The power of collective action and advocacy has helped shine a light on the issues facing minority communities and create a platform for change and progress.

As we navigate the complexities of the current political landscape, it is essential to recognize the voices and experiences of minority communities and strive towards greater inclusivity and understanding. By engaging in meaningful dialogue and promoting empathy and respect, we can work towards creating a more equitable and harmonious society for all. Politics should not be a source of division and conflict, but rather a means of bringing people together and building a brighter future for generations to come.

In conclusion, the impact of the MAGA movement on minority communities in the United States is a complex and multifaceted issue that requires careful consideration and thoughtful analysis. By acknowledging the challenges and opportunities facing minority groups, we can work towards creating a more inclusive and just society for all. Let's make politics fun again by promoting unity, diversity, and compassion in our political discourse and actions.

Trump's Policies: The Good, The Bad, and The Hilarious!

Chapter 7: Analyzing President Trumps Policies

When it comes to evaluating the key policy decisions made by President Donald Trump during his time in office, it's important to take a closer look at the impact they had on the American people. From immigration to healthcare to foreign relations, Trump's policies have sparked both controversy and praise.

One of the most notable aspects of Trump's presidency was his stance on immigration. His administration implemented strict immigration policies, such as the travel ban on several predominantly Muslim countries and the zero-tolerance policy that resulted in family separations at the border. While these policies were applauded by some for upholding national security, they were heavily criticized by others for their inhumanity and lack of compassion.

In terms of healthcare, Trump made several attempts to repeal and replace the Affordable Care Act, also known as Obamacare. Despite promises to provide a better alternative, many Americans were left uncertain about their healthcare coverage. The debate over healthcare reform continues to be a hot topic, with both sides offering different solutions to address the issue.

On the topic of foreign relations, Trump took a hardline approach with countries like North Korea and Iran. His tough stance on trade deals and international agreements, such as the Paris Climate Accord and the Iran nuclear deal, received mixed reviews. While some lauded his efforts to put America first, others criticized his isolationist policies and lack of diplomacy.

Overall, President Trump's policies have left a lasting impact on the country, shaping the political landscape for years to come. As we continue to analyze and debate the effectiveness of these policies, it's clear that they have sparked a sense of division and unity among the American people. The road ahead remains uncertain, but one thing is for sure - politics will never be the same again. When it comes to President Trump's policies, there's no shortage of debate and discussion. Let's dive into some more key decisions that have had a significant impact on the American people.

One of the most controversial aspects of Trump's presidency was his approach to environmental policy. Trump rolled back several environmental regulations, including pulling out of the Paris Climate Accord. While some saw this as a way to prioritize American jobs and industry, others criticized it for ignoring the urgent need to address climate change. The impact of these decisions on future generations remains to be seen, but it's clear that the debate over environmental policy will continue for years to come.

In terms of economic policy, Trump's administration implemented tax cuts for individuals and corporations in an effort to stimulate economic growth. While these tax cuts were welcomed by many as a way to boost the economy, others questioned the long-term effects on the national debt and income inequality. The ongoing discussion over economic policy highlights the complex balancing act that policymakers must navigate to promote prosperity for all Americans.

Another key policy area during Trump's presidency was criminal justice reform. Trump signed the First Step Act into law, which aimed to reduce mandatory minimum sentences for nonviolent offenders and improve rehabilitation programs in federal prisons. This bipartisan effort was praised for its potential to reduce recidivism rates and promote fairness in the justice system. However, some critics argued that more comprehensive reforms were needed to address systemic issues within the criminal justice system.

When it comes to education policy, Trump's administration focused on increasing school choice options and expanding access to vocational training programs. While these initiatives were applauded for providing more opportunities for students, there were concerns about the potential impact on public schools and education funding. The ongoing debate over education policy underscores the importance of finding a balance between choice and equity in the education system.

In terms of foreign policy, Trump made several controversial decisions, including withdrawing from the Iran nuclear deal and moving the U.S. embassy in Israel to Jerusalem. These moves were praised by some for showing strength and standing up for American interests, while others criticized them for fueling tensions and undermining diplomatic efforts. The impact of these decisions on the global stage remains a topic of heated debate among policymakers and analysts.

As we reflect on President Trump's policies, it's clear that they have left a lasting impact on the country. The debates over immigration, healthcare, environmental, economic, criminal justice, education, and foreign policies continue to shape the political landscape and influence the direction of our country. Regardless of where you stand on these issues, one thing is certain - politics will always be a lively and engaging topic that sparks passion and debate among the American people. Let's continue to explore, analyze, and make politics fun again!

Laughing
Our Way to
Change!

Chapter 8: Political Satire and Comedy

Late-night shows and comedians have long played a pivotal role in critiquing and dissecting political events and figures with humor. From Jon Stewart on "The Daily Show" to Seth Meyers on "Late Night," these hosts use satire and comedy to entertain audiences while shedding light on important political issues.

One of the most famous examples of political satire in recent years is Alec Baldwin's portrayal of Donald Trump on "Saturday Night Live." Baldwin's exaggerated impersonation of the former president became a cultural phenomenon, with his catchphrases like "bigly" and "covfefe" entering into the public lexicon. Through his comedic portrayal, Baldwin was able to highlight some of the more absurd aspects of Trump's presidency, bringing attention to his controversial policies and behavior.

Late-night hosts like Stephen Colbert and Trevor Noah also utilize humor to dissect political events and figures, providing a different perspective on the news of the day. Colbert, known for his character on "The Colbert Report" who parodied conservative pundits, continues to use his wit and sarcasm on "The Late Show" to critique politicians and policies. Noah, on "The Daily Show," brings his unique perspective as a South African immigrant to the political landscape, offering insights that can be both humorous and thought-provoking.

Political satire and comedy serve as a valuable tool in holding politicians accountable and engaging audiences in the political process. By using humor to highlight the absurdities and inconsistencies in politics, late-night shows and comedians are able to reach a wide audience and spark conversations about important issues. Whether it's through impression, parody, or clever commentary, these comedians provide a fresh perspective on the political landscape while making audiences laugh.

In an increasingly polarized political climate, where it can be difficult to have civil conversations about differing viewpoints, humor can break down barriers and foster understanding. Late-night shows and comedians offer a space where people can come together to laugh at the absurdities of politics, regardless of their political affiliations. This ability to unite people through laughter is a powerful tool for building bridges and promoting open dialogue in a divisive world.

As we continue to navigate the complex world of politics, it's important to remember the value of political satire and comedy in providing a unique lens through which to view current events. By exploring the world of late-night shows and comedians, we can gain a deeper understanding of the political landscape while enjoying a good laugh along the way. Stay tuned for the second half of this chapter, where we will delve deeper into the impact of political satire on our society. Now that we've explored how late-night shows and comedians use humor to dissect and critique political events and figures, let's delve deeper into the impact of political satire on our society.

Political satire has the unique ability to spark conversations, challenge beliefs, and hold powerful figures accountable in a way that traditional news media often cannot. By using humor to highlight the absurdities and inconsistencies in politics, comedians are able to shine a light on important issues and engage audiences in the political process. This engagement is crucial, especially for young people who may feel disconnected or disinterested in politics.

Late-night shows and comedians offer a fresh and entertaining perspective on the political landscape, making it more accessible and relatable to a wider audience. Through their witty commentary and clever parody, they are able to break down complex political topics into more digestible and entertaining segments. This not only educates viewers but also encourages them to think critically about the world around them.

One of the great things about political satire is its ability to transcend barriers and unite people from different backgrounds and beliefs. In a time when political divisions are becoming increasingly deep-seated, humor can be a powerful tool for bridging the gap between opposing viewpoints. By providing a space where people can come together to laugh at the absurdities of politics, late-night shows and comedians promote open dialogue and foster understanding among audiences.

Moreover, political satire has the power to challenge authority and speak truth to power in a way that can be both impactful and cathartic. Comedians like Jon Stewart, Stephen Colbert, and Trevor Noah have used their platforms to call out injustice, hypocrisy, and corruption in politics, holding politicians accountable for their actions and words. Through satire, they are able to amplify the voices of marginalized communities, shine a light on important social issues, and push for positive change in society.

In essence, political satire and comedy serve as a vital tool for democracy, encouraging citizens to question authority, challenge the status quo, and participate in civic engagement. By using humor to engage audiences in important political discussions, late-night shows and comedians are able to empower viewers to think critically, make informed decisions, and become active participants in the democratic process.

So, the next time you tune in to watch your favorite late-night show or comedian, remember the important role that political satire plays in shaping our society. Through humor and wit, these entertainers are not only making politics fun again but also inspiring us to be more engaged, informed, and active citizens in our world. Let's continue to laugh, learn, and challenge the status quo together.

YOUTH
YOUTH VOTE
YOUTH VOTE
YOUTH VOTE
YOUTH VOTE

Chapter 9: The Role of Young People in Politics

Young people have always been a driving force for change in society, and the realm of politics is no exception. In recent years, Generation Z and Millennials have been making their voices heard more than ever before, shaping the political landscape in ways that were once unimaginable.

One of the key factors behind the growing influence of young people in politics is their use of social media as a platform for activism. Platforms like Twitter, Instagram, and TikTok have provided a space for young individuals to share their views, connect with like-minded individuals, and organize events and protests. The power of social media as a tool for political change cannot be understated, as it has the potential to reach millions of people in an instant.

Additionally, young people today are more informed and engaged in political issues than ever before. With the rise of the internet and easy access to information, Generation Z and Millennials have grown up in an era where knowledge is at their fingertips. This has led to a generation that is more politically aware and active, pushing for change on issues such as climate change, gun control, and racial equality.

Moreover, young people are not afraid to challenge the status quo and demand accountability from their leaders. The passion and energy of youth have sparked movements like March for Our Lives, Black Lives Matter, and the Sunrise Movement, all of which have made significant strides in raising awareness and driving political change.

In the 2020 presidential election, young people played a pivotal role in shaping the outcome. According to the Center for Information and

Research on Civic Learning and Engagement (CIRCLE), Millennials and Generation Z made up 37% of eligible voters, making them the largest voting bloc in the country. Their turnout and engagement helped to swing key states and ultimately determine the outcome of the election.

As young people continue to make their voices heard in politics, they are challenging traditional norms and redefining the future of the country. Their passion, energy, and commitment to creating a more just and equitable society are driving forces for change. In the second half of this chapter, we will delve deeper into the specific ways in which young people are shaping politics and influencing policy decisions. But for now, let's continue to celebrate the power and impact of youth in politics, and look forward to the exciting future they are helping to create. As we delve deeper into the role of young people in politics, it's important to highlight the specific ways in which they are shaping policies and influencing decision-making at all levels of government. One of the most significant ways in which young people are making an impact is through grassroots organizing and advocacy efforts.

Young activists are not content with simply voicing their opinions on social media; they are taking to the streets, organizing marches, protests, and rallies to bring attention to the issues that matter most to them. The power of collective action cannot be underestimated, as it has the ability to capture the attention of policymakers and the public alike. Movements like Fridays for Future, started by teenage climate activist Greta Thunberg, have mobilized millions of young people around the world to demand action on climate change from their governments.

In addition to grassroots organizing, young people are also increasingly running for office themselves. A new wave of young candidates, many of whom are Millennials and members of Generation Z, are stepping up to challenge the status quo and bring fresh perspectives to the political arena. In the 2018 midterm elections, a record number of young people ran for office and won, representing a shift towards a more diverse and inclusive political landscape.

Furthermore, young people are using their voting power to hold elected officials accountable for their actions. Voter turnout among young people has been on the rise in recent elections, signaling a growing sense of responsibility and engagement in the democratic process. By showing up at the polls and casting their ballots, young voters are sending a clear message to politicians that they demand representation and action on the issues that matter most to them.

Another key way in which young people are influencing politics is through their support of political candidates and campaigns. Millennials and Generation Z are not afraid to use their voices and resources to back candidates who align with their values and priorities. Whether it's donating money, volunteering for a campaign, or simply spreading the word on social media, young people are actively engaging in the electoral process and helping to shape the outcome of elections.

In conclusion, the role of young people in politics is more important than ever before. With their passion, energy, and commitment to creating positive change, Millennials and Generation Z are redefining the future of the country and pushing for a more just and equitable society. By using their voices, organizing collective actions, running for office, and supporting political candidates, young people are making a real impact on the political landscape and shaping policy decisions that will affect future generations to come. So let's continue to celebrate the power and impact of youth in politics, and look forward to the bright future they are helping to create.

Chapter 10: The Impact of the 2020 Election

The Impact of the 2020 Election

As the dust settled from the chaotic 2020 presidential election, the American political landscape was left forever altered. With record-breaking voter turnout and a highly contested result, the aftermath of the election would have far-reaching implications for the future of American politics.

One of the most significant outcomes of the election was the historic victory of Joe Biden, who became the 46th President of the United States. His win marked a turning point in American history, as he promised to unite a deeply divided nation and bring about much-needed change. However, his victory was not without controversy, as former President Donald Trump refused to concede and made baseless claims of voter fraud.

The transition of power from the Trump administration to the Biden administration was anything but smooth. With Trump supporters storming the Capitol on January 6th, 2021 in a violent attempt to overturn the election results, the nation was left reeling. The attack on the Capitol resulted in the deaths of several individuals and showcased the deep polarization within American society.

Despite the chaos and unrest, Biden was officially sworn in as President on January 20th, 2021. His inauguration speech focused on the need for unity and healing, emphasizing the importance of coming together as a nation to tackle the pressing issues facing the country.

The 2020 election also brought about changes in Congress, with the Democrats maintaining control of the House of Representatives and gaining a narrow majority in the Senate. This shift in power would have a significant impact on the legislative agenda of the Biden administration, as he would need to work with a closely divided Congress to pass key legislation.

One of the biggest challenges facing the Biden administration would be addressing the ongoing COVID-19 pandemic. With cases continuing to rise and the economic fallout from the virus taking its toll on millions of Americans, Biden pledged to take swift action to combat the crisis. His administration would need to work quickly to distribute vaccines, provide economic relief, and implement measures to bring the pandemic under control.

As the country looked to the future, the implications of the 2020 election were clear. The political landscape had shifted, and the nation was faced with a new era of governance. The coming months and years would be crucial in determining the direction of American politics and the path forward for the country. As President Biden settled into the Oval Office, he wasted no time in taking action to address the pressing issues facing the country. One of his first priorities was tackling the ongoing COVID-19 pandemic. Biden swiftly implemented a national strategy to ramp up vaccine distribution and provide much-needed economic relief to struggling Americans. With the passage of the American Rescue Plan, a $1.9 trillion stimulus package, the Biden administration aimed to provide direct payments to individuals, support for small businesses, funding for vaccine distribution, and aid for state and local governments.

The passage of the American Rescue Plan was a significant win for the Biden administration, showcasing their ability to navigate a closely divided Congress and deliver on campaign promises. The plan received bipartisan support and was seen as a crucial step in jump-starting the economy and helping the country recover from the impacts of the pandemic.

As the Biden administration continued to push forward with their agenda, they faced challenges from both sides of the political aisle. Republicans criticized the size and scope of the stimulus package, arguing that it was bloated and contained unnecessary spending. Progressives, on the other hand, pushed for additional measures such as student loan forgiveness and Medicare for All, highlighting the divisions within the Democratic party.

Despite these challenges, Biden remained determined to deliver on his promises of unity and healing. His administration focused on working with both Democrats and Republicans to find common ground on key issues such as infrastructure, healthcare, and immigration reform. By reaching across the aisle and engaging in bipartisan collaboration, Biden hoped to bridge the divide in American politics and pave the way for a more unified future.

As the months passed, the Biden administration made progress on a number of fronts. The President signed executive orders to reverse many of the policies put in place by the Trump administration, rejoining the Paris Climate Agreement, ending the travel ban on predominantly Muslim countries, and halting construction of the border wall. These actions were met with both praise and criticism, underscoring the continued polarization within the country.

One of the most significant achievements of the Biden administration was the passage of the American Jobs Plan, a $2.3 trillion infrastructure proposal aimed at revitalizing the nation's roads, bridges, and public transportation systems. The plan also included investments in clean energy, broadband access, and workforce development, with the goal of creating millions of jobs and stimulating economic growth.

As the Biden administration continued to make progress on their legislative agenda, the impact of the 2020 election became increasingly clear. The nation had weathered a tumultuous period in its history, marked by political strife, social unrest, and a global pandemic. But through it all, the resilience of the American people shone through, demonstrating the power of democracy and the strength of a united nation.

As the chapter on the 2020 election drew to a close, the future of

American politics held both challenges and opportunities. The road ahead would be filled with twists and turns, victories and setbacks, but one thing was certain – the American people would continue to shape the course of their country, navigating the complexities of politics with optimism, perseverance, and a steadfast commitment to making politics fun again.

VOTE
LIKE YOUR
RIGHTS
DEPEND ON IT!

Chapter 11: Exploring Political Activism

Political activism comes in many different forms, each with the goal of creating change and making a difference in society. From protests and rallies to lobbying and volunteering, individuals have the power to influence political decisions and shape the world around them.

One of the most common forms of political activism is participating in protests and rallies. These events bring people together to voice their opinions, raise awareness about important issues, and demand action from elected officials. Whether it's marching in the streets or holding signs in a public space, protests are a powerful way for individuals to make their voices heard and show their support for causes they believe in.

Another form of political activism is lobbying, which involves directly contacting lawmakers and government officials to advocate for specific policies or changes. Lobbyists often work for organizations or interest groups, but individuals can also lobby their representatives by writing letters, making phone calls, or meeting with them in person. By presenting their concerns and arguments to decision-makers, individuals can influence legislation and shape public policy.

Volunteering for political campaigns and organizations is another impactful form of activism. From canvassing neighborhoods to making phone calls to hosting fundraisers, volunteers play a crucial role in helping candidates get elected and promoting important causes. By donating their time and energy, individuals can make a real difference in the political process and contribute to positive change in their communities.

Additionally, social media has become a powerful tool for political activism, allowing individuals to connect with like-minded people, share information, and mobilize support for important causes. Whether it's signing petitions, sharing articles, or starting online campaigns, social media provides a platform for individuals to raise awareness and drive change on a global scale.

Overall, political activism comes in many different forms, and each individual has the power to make a difference in their community and beyond. By participating in protests, lobbying lawmakers, volunteering for campaigns, and using social media to raise awareness, individuals can play a vital role in shaping the future of politics and creating a more just and equitable society. So, what will you do to make a difference in your community?Now that we've explored different forms of political activism, let's dive deeper into how individuals can take action and make a real impact in their communities.

One powerful way to get involved in political activism is through grassroots organizing. This involves bringing people together at the local level to work towards common goals and create change from the ground up. Grassroots movements can start small, with just a few passionate individuals working together to raise awareness and mobilize support for important issues. Through community organizing, individuals can build relationships, educate others, and create a sense of collective power that can drive meaningful change.

Another effective form of political activism is running for office. While this may seem daunting, especially for high school students, it's important to remember that anyone can be a leader and make a difference in their community. Whether it's running for student government, city council, or even Congress, taking the leap into politics can have a lasting impact on the issues that matter most to you. By representing the voices of those around you and advocating for positive change, you can shape the direction of your community and inspire others to get involved as well.

In addition to running for office, participating in local government meetings and town halls is another way to get involved in politics and make your voice heard. These public forums provide opportunities to speak directly to elected officials, express your opinions on important issues, and contribute to the decision-making process. By attending meetings, asking questions, and engaging in dialogue with policymakers, you can help shape the policies that affect your community and hold leaders accountable for their actions.

Furthermore, supporting political candidates who align with your values and beliefs is a crucial form of activism. Whether it's through donating money, volunteering for their campaign, or simply spreading the word about their platform, individuals can play a significant role in helping candidates get elected and promote positive change. By engaging in the political process and supporting candidates who prioritize issues that are important to you, you can help shape the future of politics and create a more inclusive and representative government.

Lastly, engaging in civil discourse and respectful debate is an essential part of political activism. By listening to different perspectives, engaging in dialogue with those who hold opposing views, and seeking common ground, individuals can work towards finding solutions to complex issues and fostering a more inclusive and democratic society. By approaching political conversations with an open mind, empathy, and a willingness to learn from others, you can help bridge divides, build consensus, and create a more united community.

In conclusion, political activism is a powerful tool for individuals to make a difference in their communities and shape the future of politics. Whether it's through grassroots organizing, running for office, attending town halls, supporting candidates, or engaging in civil discourse, there are countless ways for high school students and people of all ages to get involved and create positive change. So, what will you do to make politics fun again and be a force for good in your community?

Chapter 12: Media Literacy in the Digital Age

In today's digital age, the internet and social media have revolutionized the way we consume news and information. With just a few clicks, we can access a plethora of articles, videos, and social media posts that shape our understanding of the world around us. However, with this abundance of content comes the challenge of distinguishing fact from fiction.

Media literacy is crucial in the digital age, especially when it comes to politics. It's all too easy to be swayed by sensational headlines or misleading information that can distort our perception of reality. That's why it's essential to approach news and media with a critical eye, evaluating sources and fact-checking before forming opinions.

One of the key aspects of media literacy is understanding the importance of critical thinking. When consuming news online, it's important to question the source of the information, the author's credibility, and any potential biases that may be present. By approaching news with a skeptical mindset, we can sift through the noise and distinguish credible information from misinformation.

Another crucial aspect of media literacy is evaluating sources. Not all sources are created equal, and it's essential to consider the credibility of the outlets we rely on for news. Fact-checking organizations like Snopes and PolitiFact can help us verify the accuracy of information and identify fake news.

In the era of social media, it's equally important to be mindful of the echo chamber effect. We tend to follow and engage with content that aligns with our beliefs, creating a bubble of like-minded individuals. To combat this, it's essential to seek out diverse perspectives and challenge our own viewpoints to foster a more well-rounded understanding of political issues.

By honing our media literacy skills, we can become more informed and active participants in the political landscape. As we navigate the digital age, critical thinking and evaluating sources are crucial tools that empower us to separate truth from fiction and make informed decisions. In the realm of politics, where misinformation runs rampant, media literacy is a powerful weapon against deception and manipulation. Now that we've covered the basics of media literacy in the digital age, let's delve deeper into some practical tips and strategies to help you navigate the overwhelming landscape of online news and social media.

One important skill to develop is the ability to fact-check information before sharing it or forming opinions. With the rise of fake news and misinformation, it's essential to verify the accuracy of sources before spreading false information. Fact-checking websites like Snopes and PolitiFact can be valuable tools in determining the credibility of news stories and rumors. Remember, just because something confirms your beliefs or seems too outrageous to be true, doesn't mean it's accurate.

Another key aspect of media literacy is understanding the power of algorithms in shaping the content you see online. Social media platforms like Facebook and Twitter use algorithms to curate your news feed based on your browsing history and interactions. This can create a filter bubble, where you are only exposed to content that aligns with your existing beliefs. To break out of this bubble, actively seek out diverse sources of information and engage with people who hold different perspectives.

It's also important to be aware of the prevalence of clickbait and sensational headlines designed to draw you in and trigger an emotional response. Before sharing an article or reacting to a post, take a moment to critically evaluate the content and consider the motivations behind its creation. Is the headline misleading or exaggerated? Are there any hidden agendas at play? By approaching news with a healthy dose of skepticism, you can avoid falling victim to manipulative tactics.

Additionally, be mindful of the concept of "confirmation bias," which refers to the tendency to seek out information that confirms our existing beliefs while ignoring or dismissing evidence that challenges them. To combat this cognitive bias, make a conscious effort to expose yourself to diverse viewpoints and actively seek out information that may challenge your assumptions. This can help you develop a more well-rounded understanding of complex political issues and make more informed decisions.

In conclusion, media literacy in the digital age is crucial for navigating the complex landscape of online news and social media. By honing your critical thinking skills, evaluating sources, fact-checking information, and seeking out diverse perspectives, you can become a more informed and discerning consumer of media. Remember, in the realm of politics, where deception and manipulation abound, being media literate is a powerful tool for uncovering the truth and making sense of the world around you. So, next time you come across a provocative headline or a controversial post, take a step back, think critically, and approach it with a discerning eye. Together, we can make politics fun again by staying informed, engaged, and empowered.

Chapter 13: From the Classroom to Capitol Hill

As we transition from the classroom to Capitol Hill, it's important for students to understand the power they hold to make a difference in politics. Advocacy and activism are not just reserved for adults - young people have a vital role to play in shaping the future of our country.

One way for students to get involved in politics is through student government. Whether it's running for class president or joining the student council, these positions provide opportunities to practice leadership skills and make decisions that impact the school community. By participating in student government, students can learn how the political process works and gain valuable experience that can be applied to future endeavors in politics.

Another way for students to advocate for causes they believe in is through activism. This can take many forms, from organizing a protest on campus to starting a petition to address a social issue. By speaking out and taking action, students can raise awareness about important topics and push for change in their schools, communities, and beyond.

Additionally, participating in political campaigns and volunteering for candidates is a great way for students to get hands-on experience in politics. By helping with phone banks, canvassing neighborhoods, or organizing events, students can learn about the campaign process and see firsthand how elections are won and lost. This involvement can also lead to networking opportunities and connections that may prove valuable in the future.

Furthermore, engaging in political discussions and debates with peers can help students refine their arguments and understand different perspectives. By listening to and engaging with others who have differing opinions, students can develop critical thinking skills and learn how to communicate effectively in a political context. These skills are essential for anyone looking to make an impact in the political arena.

Overall, students have the power to make politics fun again by getting involved, advocating for causes they believe in, and making their voices heard. By taking action and participating in the political process, young people can shape the future of our country and create a more inclusive and representative democracy for all. The possibilities are endless - the only limit is your imagination. Now that we've explored the various ways students can get involved in politics, let's delve deeper into the impact they can have on shaping the political landscape. From organizing rallies to engaging in debates, students have the ability to make a lasting impression on the issues that matter most to them.

One powerful way students can advocate for causes they believe in is through social media. Platforms like Twitter, Instagram, and TikTok provide a stage for young voices to be heard and spark conversations about important topics. By sharing their thoughts, experiences, and opinions online, students can reach a wider audience and build support for their causes. Whether it's using a trending hashtag to raise awareness about climate change or sharing personal stories to shed light on social injustices, social media can be a powerful tool for creating change.

Another avenue for student involvement in politics is through community organizing. By partnering with local organizations and grassroots movements, students can engage with their communities and work towards solutions to pressing issues. Whether it's advocating for better education funding, supporting marginalized groups, or promoting environmental sustainability, community organizing allows students to make a tangible impact in their neighborhoods and beyond.

Furthermore, attending political events and town hall meetings can provide valuable insights into the workings of government and the concerns of constituents. By listening to elected officials, engaging in discussions, and asking questions, students can gain a better understanding of the issues facing their communities and the policies that can address them. This firsthand experience can inspire students to take action and advocate for meaningful change in their local and state governments.

In addition, volunteering with advocacy groups and non-profit organizations can offer students the opportunity to contribute to causes they are passionate about. Whether it's volunteering at a food bank, participating in a clean-up project, or working on a voter registration drive, students can make a difference in their communities and support initiatives that align with their values. These experiences can also help students build connections with like-minded individuals and expand their knowledge of social issues.

Lastly, participating in youth-led initiatives and campaigns can empower students to effect change on a larger scale. By joining movements like the March for Our Lives or the Sunrise Movement, students can amplify their voices and advocate for policies that reflect their concerns. Through collective action and solidarity, young people can make a significant impact on the political landscape and inspire change at the national level.

In conclusion, students have a unique opportunity to make politics fun again by engaging in advocacy, activism, and community involvement. By utilizing their voices, skills, and passions, young people can play a pivotal role in shaping the future of our democracy and creating a more equitable and inclusive society for all. So, let's roll up our sleeves, get involved, and make a difference - the future is in our hands!

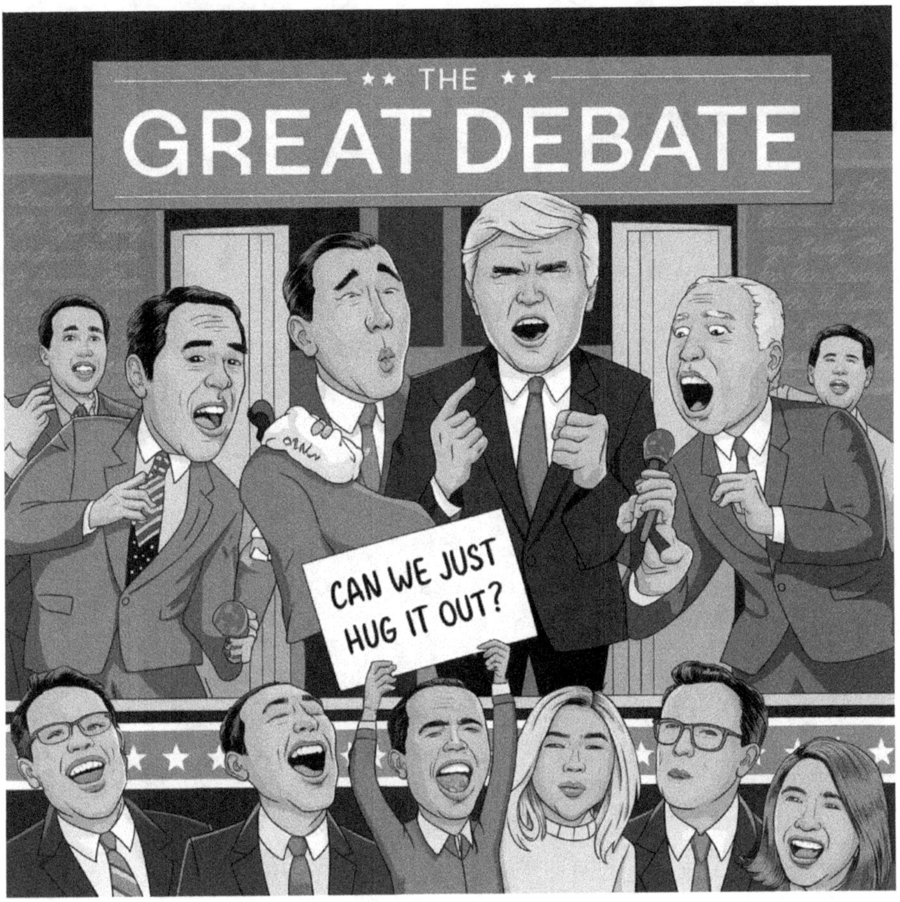
THE
GREAT DEBATE
CAN WE JUST HUG IT OUT?

Chapter 14: Political Debates and Discourse

Political debates and discourse are essential components of a healthy democracy. They allow individuals to express their opinions, challenge each other's ideas, and ultimately come to a better understanding of complex political issues. However, in recent years, political debates have become increasingly polarized and divisive, with individuals on opposite sides of the political spectrum often resorting to personal attacks and inflammatory rhetoric.

But it doesn't have to be this way. Debating political issues can and should be a respectful and constructive exercise. Here are some tips on how to engage in political debates in a more productive and respectful manner:

First and foremost, it's important to approach political debates with an open mind. Remember that everyone is entitled to their own opinions and perspectives, even if they differ from your own. Listen actively to what the other person is saying, and try to understand their reasoning behind their beliefs.

When presenting your own arguments, stick to the facts and avoid using inflammatory language or personal attacks. Focus on the issue at hand, and try to present your arguments in a logical and coherent manner. Avoid strawman arguments or misrepresenting your opponent's position – instead, engage with their actual points and provide counterarguments based on evidence and logic.

It's also important to stay calm and composed during political debates. Emotions can run high when discussing contentious political issues, but getting angry or defensive will only escalate the situation. Remember that the goal of political debates is not to "win" or prove the other person wrong, but to engage in a constructive dialogue and exchange ideas.

Lastly, be willing to admit when you are wrong or when you don't have all the answers. It's okay to change your opinion or acknowledge that you need to do more research on a particular issue. Humility and intellectual honesty are key components of respectful political discourse.

By following these tips and approaching political debates with an open mind, a focus on facts, emotional intelligence, and intellectual honesty, we can make political debates fun and engaging again. So let's strive to foster a culture of respectful political discourse and make debates a platform for education and understanding rather than division and conflict. Now that we've covered the basics of engaging in political debates with respect and constructiveness, let's delve deeper into the art of discourse. One important aspect to keep in mind is the power of empathy. Empathy involves putting yourself in someone else's shoes and trying to see things from their perspective. By practicing empathy during political debates, you can better understand where the other person is coming from and find common ground to build upon.

Another key element of productive political discourse is active listening. This means giving the person speaking your full attention, really hearing what they have to say, and responding thoughtfully. By actively listening, you can show respect for the other person's opinions and create a more meaningful dialogue.

It's also important to be mindful of your body language during political debates. Non-verbal cues such as eye contact, facial expressions, and gestures can have a big impact on how your arguments are perceived. By maintaining good eye contact, nodding in agreement, and avoiding defensive postures, you can convey openness and receptiveness to the other person's ideas.

Furthermore, it's essential to do your homework before engaging in political debates. Make sure you have a solid understanding of the topic at hand, do your research, and come prepared with facts and evidence to support your arguments. This will not only strengthen your position but also demonstrate to others that you are knowledgeable and informed.

In addition, be mindful of the language you use during political debates. Avoid derogatory or inflammatory language that can escalate tensions and derail productive conversations. Instead, choose your words carefully, speak respectfully, and focus on the issue at hand rather than resorting to personal attacks.

Lastly, don't be afraid to walk away from a heated discussion if it becomes unproductive or too emotionally charged. It's okay to take a step back, cool off, and revisit the conversation at a later time when emotions have settled down. Remember that the goal of political debates is not to "win" but to have a meaningful exchange of ideas and learn from each other.

By adopting these strategies and approaches to political debates, we can create a more positive and inclusive discourse that fosters understanding, empathy, and cooperation. Let's make politics fun again by engaging in respectful and constructive conversations that bring us closer together rather than drive us apart. Now go out there and have some productive and enjoyable political debates!

Future
Vision!

Chapter 15: The Future of the Republican Party

The Future of the Republican Party

As we look towards the future of the Republican Party post-Trump, it's important to acknowledge the significant impact that the former president has had on the GOP. Trump's presidency was marked by controversy, divisiveness, and a populist approach to politics that resonated with many Americans. His unorthodox style and willingness to challenge the establishment energized a fervent base of supporters, but also alienated many traditional Republicans.

With Trump no longer in office, the GOP finds itself at a crossroads. Some believe that the party will continue to embrace Trumpism, with candidates who align themselves closely with the former president's policies and rhetoric. Others argue that the party needs to move away from Trump's divisive tactics and focus on a more inclusive message that appeals to a wider range of voters.

One thing is certain - the Republican Party is in the midst of a soul-searching moment. The 2020 election results revealed deep divisions within the party, with some Republicans distancing themselves from Trump in order to appeal to moderate voters, while others doubled down on their support for the former president.

Moving forward, it will be crucial for the GOP to find a balance between appealing to Trump's base and expanding its reach to attract new voters. The party will need to address key issues such as immigration, healthcare, and climate change in order to remain relevant in a rapidly changing political landscape.

The future of the Republican Party will have profound implications for American politics as a whole. Whether the GOP chooses to embrace Trumpism or move in a new direction, the decisions made in the coming years will shape the party's identity and influence its ability to win elections.

As we look ahead to the next chapter in the Republican Party's history, one thing is clear - the only constant in politics is change. And with change comes the opportunity for growth and evolution. The GOP must navigate the challenges ahead with a clear vision and a commitment to principles that will resonate with a diverse and changing electorate. Only time will tell what the future holds for the Grand Old Party. Now that we have explored the impact of Trump on the GOP and speculated on the future direction of the Republican Party, let's dive deeper into what the post-Trump era could look like and the potential implications for American politics.

One possible scenario is that the Republican Party continues to embrace Trumpism, with candidates and lawmakers closely aligning themselves with the former president's policies and rhetoric. This could mean a continued focus on issues such as immigration reform, tax cuts, and deregulation, which were hallmarks of Trump's time in office. This approach may appeal to the more conservative base of the party, but could also further alienate moderate and independent voters who may be turned off by Trump's divisive style.

On the other hand, there is a growing faction within the GOP that believes the party needs to move away from Trump's influence and chart a new course. This group argues that the party should focus on building a more inclusive message that appeals to a broader range of voters, including minorities, women, and young people. This approach could help the Republican Party expand its electoral base and compete more effectively in future elections.

One key issue that the GOP will need to address moving forward is the role of Trump himself. While he remains a powerful figure within the party, there are signs that some Republicans are eager to break with the former president and forge a new path. The 2020 election results, in which Trump lost the popular vote and the electoral college, have prompted many in the party to reassess their allegiance to Trump and consider alternative leadership.

In addition to the question of Trump's influence, the Republican Party will also need to confront pressing policy issues in the coming years. Immigration reform, healthcare, and climate change are all issues that will require careful consideration and strategic planning. The GOP will need to develop clear and coherent policy positions on these issues in order to remain relevant and competitive in the political landscape.

Ultimately, the future of the Republican Party will depend on how the party navigates these challenges and adapts to a changing political environment. The decisions made in the coming years will shape the party's identity and influence its ability to win elections. It is a pivotal moment for the GOP, and the choices that party leaders make will have far-reaching implications for American politics as a whole.

As we look ahead to the future of the Republican Party, one thing is certain - the only constant in politics is change. The GOP has an opportunity to grow and evolve in response to the challenges of the post-Trump era, and it will be up to party leaders and members to seize that opportunity and chart a new course for the Republican Party. The road ahead may be uncertain, but one thing is clear - the future of the GOP is in the hands of those who are willing to embrace change and lead the party into a new era of politics.

Progress through Time!
Progress through Time!
Progress through Time!

Chapter 16: The Democratic Party's Evolution

The Democratic Party has undergone significant evolution throughout its history, shaping its current positions on key issues. From its origins in the Democratic-Republican Party founded by Thomas Jefferson in the early 19th century, to the modern iteration we see today, the party has adapted to the changing political landscape of the United States.

One of the most notable shifts for the Democratic Party occurred during the Civil Rights Movement of the 1960s. Previously, the party had strongholds in the Southern states, where it represented the interests of white conservative voters. However, as the party embraced civil rights and equality for all Americans regardless of race, it faced significant push-back from its traditional base.

This shift led to a realignment within the party, with conservative Democrats in the South defecting to the Republican Party, while the Democratic Party became more diverse and inclusive. The party's strong stance on civil rights and social justice has become a core value, influencing its positions on issues such as affirmative action, LGBTQ rights, and criminal justice reform.

In recent years, the Democratic Party has also taken a more progressive stance on economic issues. The party has embraced policies such as increasing the minimum wage, expanding access to healthcare, and addressing income inequality. The rise of progressive leaders like Bernie Sanders and Alexandria Ocasio-Cortez has pushed the party to the left on economic matters, advocating for bold solutions to address the challenges facing working-class Americans.

On foreign policy, the Democratic Party has traditionally been more interventionist, supporting military interventions and international alliances. However, there is a growing faction within the party that is more skeptical of American military involvement abroad, advocating for a more restrained and diplomatic approach to foreign affairs.

With the election of Joe Biden as President in 2020, the Democratic Party has continued to navigate these evolving positions on key issues. Biden has sought to bridge the divide between the party's progressive and moderate wings, focusing on policies like infrastructure investment, climate change mitigation, and healthcare reform.

As the Democratic Party continues to evolve and adapt to the changing political landscape, it faces challenges in maintaining its diverse coalition of supporters. However, with a renewed focus on inclusivity, social justice, and economic progress, the party remains a powerful force in American politics.

Stay tuned for the second half of this chapter, where we will delve deeper into the current positions and challenges facing the Democratic Party in the 21st century. Now, let's take a closer look at some of the current positions and challenges facing the Democratic Party in the 21st century.

One of the key issues that the Democratic Party has been focusing on is climate change. With the growing threat of global warming and environmental degradation, Democrats have been advocating for bold action to address this urgent issue. From supporting renewable energy initiatives to rejoining the Paris Climate Agreement, the party has made combating climate change a top priority. This aligns with the views of many young voters, who are increasingly concerned about the impact of climate change on the planet.

Another important issue that the Democratic Party is grappling with is healthcare reform. The party has long been a proponent of expanding access to affordable healthcare for all Americans. The passage of the Affordable Care Act (ACA) under President Obama was a major step forward in this regard, but there are still challenges to overcome. Democrats are working to strengthen the ACA, expand Medicaid, and lower prescription drug costs to ensure that all Americans have access to quality healthcare.

Income inequality is also a major focus for the Democratic Party. With the gap between the rich and the poor continuing to widen, Democrats are advocating for policies that promote economic fairness and opportunity for all. This includes raising the minimum wage, providing paid family leave, and implementing tax reforms that benefit working families. By addressing income inequality, the party hopes to create a more equitable society where everyone has a chance to succeed.

On the international stage, the Democratic Party is grappling with how to approach foreign policy in a changing world. While some Democrats are more skeptical of American military intervention abroad, others still support a strong presence on the global stage. Finding a balance between national security and diplomacy is a key challenge for the party as it navigates complex geopolitical issues.

In addition to these policy issues, the Democratic Party also faces challenges in maintaining its diverse coalition of supporters. With a wide range of views and priorities among its members, the party must find common ground to unite behind key initiatives. This includes bridging the gap between progressive and moderate factions, addressing the needs of different demographic groups, and engaging with voters across the political spectrum.

Despite these challenges, the Democratic Party remains a powerful force in American politics, driven by a commitment to inclusivity, social justice, and economic progress. By staying true to its core values and adapting to the changing political landscape, the party continues to shape the future of the country.

In conclusion, the Democratic Party has come a long way from its origins in the early 19th century. Through evolution and adaptation, the party has remained a vital player in American politics, advocating for progressive policies and social change. As the party navigates the challenges of the 21st century, it will be interesting to see how it continues to make politics fun again for all who are passionate about the future of our country.

WHY NOT US?

Chapter 17: The Role of Third Parties in American Politics

When it comes to American politics, the two-party system has dominated the landscape for centuries. However, third parties have always played a significant role in shaping the political discourse and offering alternative viewpoints. From the Green Party to the Libertarian Party, these smaller parties have faced numerous challenges in trying to compete with the Democrats and Republicans.

One of the biggest challenges faced by third parties in American politics is the lack of media coverage and exposure. With the two major parties dominating the airwaves and news headlines, it can be difficult for third-party candidates to get their message out to the public. Without the same level of funding and resources as the major parties, third parties often struggle to gain visibility and attract voters.

Another challenge for third parties is the winner-takes-all system in place for most elections in the US. This system makes it difficult for third-party candidates to win seats in Congress or other government positions, as they often have to compete against well-established candidates from the major parties. This can be discouraging for third-party supporters, who may feel like their votes are wasted if their candidate does not win.

Despite these challenges, there are also opportunities for third parties to make an impact in American politics. One major opportunity is the growing disillusionment with the two-party system among voters. Many Americans are fed up with the gridlock and partisanship in Washington, leading them to seek out alternative options. This presents an opening for third parties to attract disaffected voters and offer a different vision for the country.

Additionally, third parties can play a crucial role in pushing the major parties to address certain issues or adopt certain policies. By raising awareness about important issues and forcing the major parties to take notice, third parties can have a significant influence on the political agenda. Even if they do not win elections, third parties can still make a difference by shaping the debate and bringing attention to overlooked issues.

Overall, the role of third parties in American politics is complex and multifaceted. While they face many challenges in trying to compete with the Democrats and Republicans, third parties also have unique opportunities to make a lasting impact on the political landscape. As we delve deeper into the world of third parties, we will explore how these smaller parties navigate the rough waters of American politics and strive to make their voices heard.Now, let's take a closer look at some of the specific third parties that have made waves in American politics.

One of the most well-known third parties is the Libertarian Party, which advocates for limited government intervention in both economic and social matters. Founded in 1971, the Libertarian Party has fielded candidates for president, Congress, and various state and local offices. While they have yet to win a significant number of seats, they have garnered a dedicated following of supporters who believe in their platform of individual freedom and limited government.

Another notable third party is the Green Party, which focuses on environmental issues, social justice, and nonviolence. Founded in 2001, the Green Party has also run candidates at various levels of government, including multiple presidential campaigns. While they have not had much success in winning elections, the Green Party has been able to bring attention to important environmental and social justice issues that may have otherwise been overlooked.

In addition to the Libertarian and Green Parties, there are a number of other third parties that have played a role in American politics, such as the Constitution Party, the Reform Party, and the Independent Party. Each of these parties brings a unique perspective and set of values to the political table, providing voters with alternative options to the two major parties.

Despite their struggles to compete with the Democrats and Republicans, third parties continue to have a significant impact on the American political landscape. By raising awareness about important issues, pushing the major parties to address key concerns, and offering alternative viewpoints, third parties play a crucial role in shaping the political discourse and challenging the status quo.

So, how can we make third parties more successful in American politics? One potential solution is to reform the electoral system to make it more inclusive of third-party candidates. Implementing ranked-choice voting, for example, could help third parties gain more support by allowing voters to rank their choices in order of preference.

Another way to support third parties is for voters to educate themselves on the platforms and candidates of these smaller parties. By taking the time to learn about the positions and values of third-party candidates, voters can make more informed decisions at the ballot box and help to break the stranglehold of the two-party system.

In conclusion, while third parties face numerous challenges in competing with the Democrats and Republicans, they also offer unique opportunities to bring new ideas and perspectives to the political arena. By supporting and advocating for third parties, we can help to make American politics more diverse, inclusive, and representative of the diverse views and values of the American people. Let's continue to explore the world of third parties and see how they can continue to make politics fun again.

Chapter 18: Balancing Political Activism and Self-Care

In today's fast-paced world, it's easy to get caught up in the whirlwind of political activism. With social media constantly bombarding us with news and opinions, it can be overwhelming to stay engaged while also prioritizing our mental and emotional well-being. But fear not, dear reader, for there are ways to balance the two without sacrificing your sanity.

One key strategy is to set boundaries for yourself. It's important to know when to unplug and take a break from the relentless stream of information. This doesn't mean you have to disengage completely, but rather, make a conscious effort to limit your exposure to political content when it becomes too much. Give your mind a chance to rest and recharge before diving back into the fray.

Another way to stay engaged in politics while practicing self-care is to find a support system. Surround yourself with like-minded individuals who share your passion for change. Whether it's through online forums, local activist groups, or simply having meaningful conversations with friends and family, having a network of support can help you navigate the complexities of political activism without feeling isolated or overwhelmed.

Additionally, don't be afraid to prioritize your own well-being. Self-care is not selfish – it's essential for your mental and emotional health. Take time for yourself to do things that bring you joy, whether it's reading a book, going for a walk, or indulging in your favorite hobby. Remember, you can't pour from an empty cup, so make sure to take care of yourself first before trying to change the world.

Lastly, remember to practice mindfulness in your political activism. Be aware of how certain issues and discussions affect your mental and emotional state. If you find yourself getting too worked up or stressed out, take a step back and reassess your approach. It's okay to take a breather and come back with a fresh perspective.

So, dear reader, as you navigate the murky waters of political activism, remember to prioritize your mental and emotional well-being. Set boundaries, find a support system, prioritize self-care, and practice mindfulness. By taking care of yourself first, you'll be better equipped to make a difference in the world. And with that, let's dive into the second half of this chapter, where we'll explore even more strategies for balancing political activism and self-care. Now that we've covered some key strategies for balancing political activism and self-care, lets dive into a few more tips to help you navigate the world of politics without losing your mind.

One important aspect to consider is the power of perspective. Sometimes, we can get so caught up in the negativity and divisiveness of politics that we forget to step back and see the bigger picture. Remember that change takes time, and progress is often slow. By keeping a long-term perspective and focusing on the victories, no matter how small, you can maintain a sense of hope and motivation in your activism.

Another helpful strategy is to practice gratitude. It can be easy to focus on everything that is wrong in the world, but taking the time to appreciate the positive aspects of your life can help shift your mindset and keep you grounded. Whether its writing in a gratitude journal, meditating on the things you are thankful for, or simply expressing appreciation to those around you, practicing gratitude can be a powerful tool in maintaining your mental and emotional well-being.

In addition, don't be afraid to take a step back when you need to. Its okay to prioritize your own well-being and step away from political activism for a while if its becoming too overwhelming. Take a break, recharge, and come back with a fresh perspective when you feel ready. Remember, you are not alone in this fight, and its important to take care of yourself so that you can continue to make a difference in the long run.

Lastly, remember to celebrate your wins, no matter how small they may seem. Whether its a successful protest, a policy change in your community, or simply educating someone on an important issue, take time to acknowledge and celebrate the progress you have made. Recognizing your achievements can boost your morale and keep you motivated to continue your political activism in a healthy and sustainable way.

So, dear reader, as you continue on your journey of political activism, remember to prioritize your mental and emotional well-being. Set boundaries, find support, practice self-care, stay mindful, maintain perspective, practice gratitude, take breaks when needed, and celebrate your wins. By taking care of yourself first, youll be better equipped to make a positive impact on the world around you. Keep up the good work, and remember to have fun along the way!

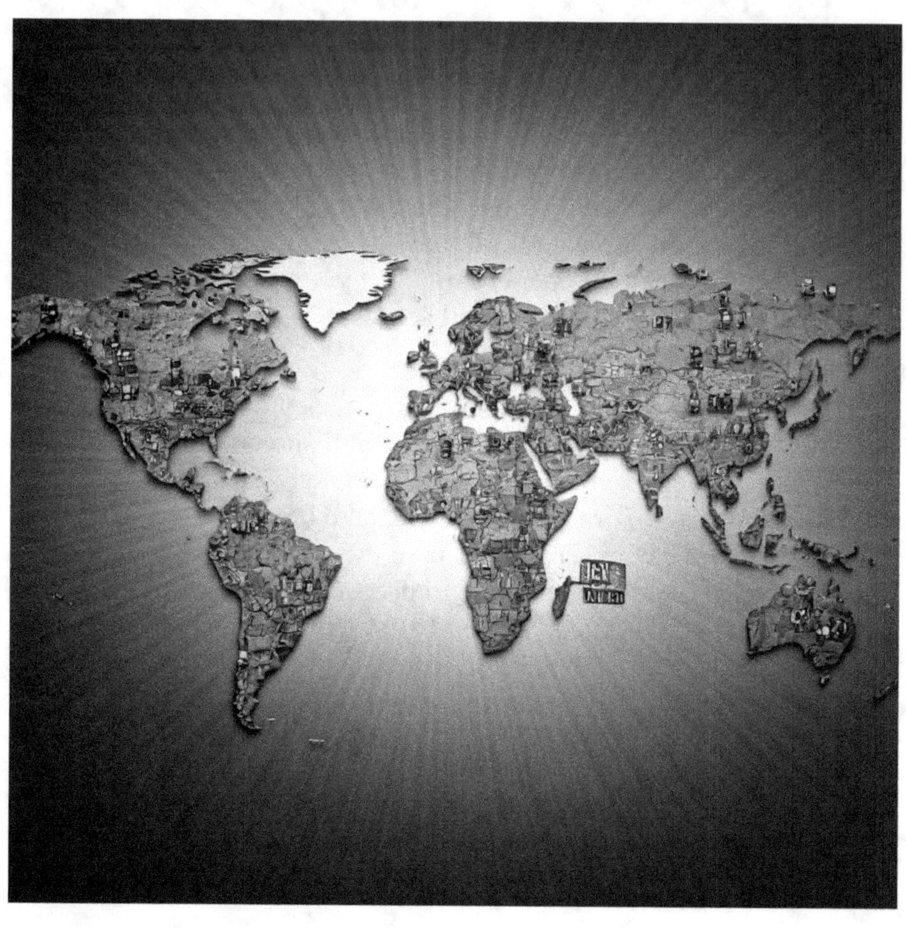

Chapter 19: The Global Impact of the MAGA Movement

The global impact of the MAGA movement cannot be understated. While the movement itself is centered around America, its influence has resonated with international audiences and had far-reaching implications on global politics.

One of the key ways in which the MAGA movement has influenced global politics is through its emphasis on nationalism and populism. The idea of putting America first and prioritizing the interests of the nation over global cooperation has struck a chord with many around the world who feel disillusioned with the current state of affairs. This sentiment has been echoed in countries like Brazil, Italy, and the Philippines, where leaders have adopted a similar nationalist approach to governance.

Additionally, the rhetoric and policies espoused by the MAGA movement have sparked debates and conversations on a global scale. Issues such as immigration, trade, and international relations have been heavily influenced by the America-first mentality championed by the movement. The push for stricter border controls, tariffs on imports, and renegotiation of trade agreements have set a new precedent in global politics and have caused ripple effects in many countries.

Furthermore, the rise of populism and anti-establishment sentiment that the MAGA movement embodies has had implications for democracies around the world. Countries like Hungary, Poland, and Turkey have seen the erosion of democratic norms and the rise of strongman leaders who prioritize their own power over the rule of law. The success of Donald Trump in the United States has emboldened populist leaders in other countries to follow suit and challenge the status quo.

Overall, the global impact of the MAGA movement is undeniable. Its message of putting America first and prioritizing national interests has resonated with people around the world who feel marginalized by globalization and frustrated with the political establishment. As we continue to see the effects of this movement play out on the international stage, it is clear that the legacy of Make America Great Again will be felt for years to come. The global impact of the MAGA movement has not only influenced politics, but also sparked cultural shifts and conversations around the world. The rise of America-first policies and the emphasis on national sovereignty have challenged traditional alliances and forced countries to reevaluate their relationships with the United States. This shift in global dynamics has caused tensions among allies and adversaries alike, as countries navigate the new landscape created by the MAGA movement.

One of the key areas where the influence of the MAGA movement can be seen is in the realm of international trade. The imposition of tariffs on imports and the push for renegotiation of trade agreements have caused disruptions in global markets and strained relationships with trading partners. Countries like China, Canada, and the European Union have been forced to respond to the protectionist measures implemented by the United States, leading to retaliatory actions and trade disputes that have reverberated around the world.

Additionally, the America-first mentality championed by the MAGA movement has had implications for international relations and diplomacy. The emphasis on unilateral decision-making and the prioritization of national interests over global cooperation have eroded trust in traditional alliances and institutions. The United States' withdrawal from international agreements such as the Paris Climate Accord and the Iran nuclear deal has further isolated the country on the world stage and raised concerns about its commitment to upholding global norms and values.

Moreover, the rise of nationalism and populism fueled by the MAGA movement has emboldened authoritarian leaders and dictators to crack down on dissent and suppress opposition. Countries like Russia, North Korea, and Venezuela have capitalized on the rhetoric of "America first" to justify their own actions and undermine democratic principles. The erosion of democratic norms and the rise of autocratic regimes pose a threat to global stability and human rights, as leaders exploit nationalist sentiments to consolidate their power and silence dissent.

Despite the divisive and polarizing nature of the MAGA movement, it has sparked important conversations about the role of nationalism in modern politics and the impact of populism on democratic institutions. The legacy of Make America Great Again will continue to shape global politics for years to come, as countries grapple with the consequences of putting national interests above all else. As we navigate the complexities of a world influenced by the MAGA movement, it is imperative that we remain vigilant in protecting democratic values and upholding the principles of freedom and equality for all.

Unity
Progress

Chapter 20: Building a Better Political Future

As we reflect on the lessons learned from the MAGA movement, one thing becomes clear: politics doesn't have to be a dirty word. It can be exciting, engaging, and yes, even fun. But in order to build a better political future, we need to start by creating a more inclusive and equitable landscape for everyone.

One of the key takeaways from the MAGA movement is the power of grassroots organizing. Whether you agree with their politics or not, it's hard to deny the impact they had on the political landscape. From rallies to door-knocking campaigns, they mobilized their base in a way that hadn't been seen in years. So, how can we harness that energy and enthusiasm for the greater good?

First and foremost, we need to make sure that everyone feels heard and represented in our political system. That means reaching out to communities that have been marginalized or ignored in the past. It means listening to their concerns and working together to find solutions that benefit everyone, not just a select few.

Additionally, we need to prioritize transparency and accountability in our political leaders. The MAGA movement thrived on the idea of draining the swamp and getting rid of corruption in Washington. While their methods may have been questionable at times, the underlying message resonated with many people. Moving forward, we need to hold our elected officials to a higher standard and demand that they act in the best interests of the people, not themselves.

Finally, we need to focus on building bridges, not walls. The divisiveness that has defined our political landscape in recent years has only served to deepen the rifts between us. If we truly want to create a better future for all, we need to come together and find common ground. That means putting aside our differences and working towards a shared vision of a more inclusive and equitable society.

In the end, building a better political future is going to take work. It's not going to happen overnight, and it's not going to be easy. But if we can learn from the lessons of the past and commit ourselves to creating a more inclusive and equitable political landscape, then there's no limit to what we can achieve. Let's make politics fun again, and let's create a future that we can all be proud of. Now that we've laid the groundwork for building a better political future, let's dive deeper into how we can continue to make politics more engaging and inclusive for everyone. One of the key ways we can do this is by encouraging young people to get involved in the political process. After all, they are the future leaders of tomorrow, and their voices deserve to be heard.

One way to inspire young people to get involved is by making civics education a priority in schools. By teaching students about the importance of government, elections, and how to be an active participant in the political process, we can empower them to become informed and engaged citizens. After all, knowledge is power, and the more we educate our youth about the inner workings of our political system, the better equipped they will be to advocate for change in the future.

Another way to build a better political future is by fostering a culture of respect and open dialogue. In today's polarized political climate, it's all too easy to resort to personal attacks and divisive rhetoric. But if we want to move forward as a society, we need to learn how to disagree respectfully and listen to differing perspectives. By engaging in civil discourse and finding common ground, we can bridge the gap between opposing viewpoints and work towards solutions that benefit everyone.

Additionally, we must continue to hold our elected officials accountable for their actions. Transparency and integrity are essential components of a functioning democracy, and it's up to us as citizens to demand that our leaders act with honesty and integrity. By staying informed about what our elected officials are doing, holding them accountable for their promises, and speaking out against corruption and abuse of power, we can ensure that our government remains accountable to the people it serves.

Furthermore, we must continue to prioritize inclusivity and diversity in our political landscape. This means actively seeking out and amplifying the voices of those who have been historically marginalized or underrepresented in politics. By creating space for a diverse range of perspectives and experiences, we can ensure that all voices are heard and valued in the decision-making process.

In conclusion, building a better political future is a collective effort that requires each and every one of us to do our part. By prioritizing inclusivity, accountability, respect, and education, we can create a more vibrant and equitable political landscape that engages and empowers all members of our society. So let's roll up our sleeves, put on our thinking caps, and get to work building a future that we can all be proud of. Together, we can make politics fun again and create a better world for generations to come.

Resources and Recommended Tools

Before you dive into the treasure trove of resources below, I want to be transparent with you. Some of the links I've included might be affiliate links, which means that if you decide to use them, I might earn a small commission—just a little extra to keep the lights on. However, not all links are affiliate, and regardless of that, I only recommend tools and resources that I genuinely believe in and have found valuable in my own experience with trusts. These resources are designed to assist you on your journey, and I hope you find them as useful as I have!

Amazon Affiliate Link:
When you purchase through this link, I earn a small commission at no extra cost to you. The price remains the same, but your support helps keep this content coming. Thank you!

https://amzn.to/3NbM0RD

The Nerd Picker Blog

http://nerdpicker.com

Proven Amazon Course
The Very Best Amazon Training Course!

http://provenamazoncourse.biz

My Facebook Biz page

http://www.facebook.com/TheNerdpicker

My Facebook Profile Page

http://facebook.com/michael.markuson

Silent Sales Machine Radio Podcast

http://bit.ly/SilentJim-Podcast

Free Facebook group for Amazon and Reselling (MST)

Pretty amazing group of over 75K members!

https://bit.ly/MST-facebookgroup

I have 2 Youtube Channels – Please Subscribe to both (thanks)

https://www.youtube.com/@MichaelMarkusonTheNerdpicker

and

https://www.youtube.com/c/MichaelMarkuson

Backup your Data! Important!

https://bit.ly/backitupbiz

My Final Recommendation!

It is pretty amazing. Check it out on the next page...
Thanks

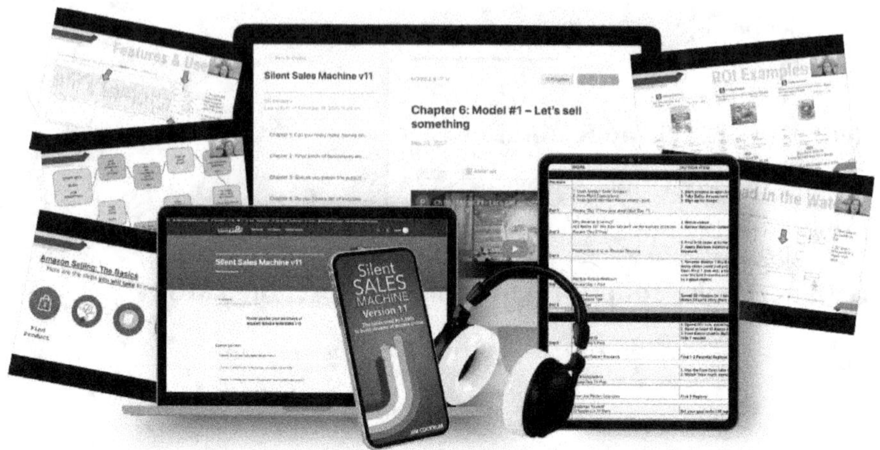

The complete step by step guide to create an 'Amazon Replens' business for $17.00 (95% off)
https://ko296.isrefer.com/go/ssmb/MMarkuson/

Here is what's included:

1. #1 Best Selling Book 'Silent Sales Machine', endorsed by Dave Ramsey, and read by over 1 million globally ($19 value).

2. The Amazon 101 Course with every detail needed (with step-by-step instructions) to get your first sale on Amazon ($297 value).

3. The Fast Start Guide that breaks down every step into an actionable 30 day plan to get to your first sale as fast as possible ($47 value).

You'll also get to interact with hundreds of students in our private Facebook group who replaced their 9-5 using this exact strategy.

(Total value: $363).

Individually, we sell these items everyday in our store at this amount.

But our goal is to continue to be the largest community of Amazon sellers in the world, and collect even more success stories.

So Jim and his team and I decided to offer this bundle for only $17.00 (95% off), at this link:

https://ko296.isrefer.com/go/ssmb/MMarkuson/

Students using this method tell Jim's team all the time…

Their biggest regret was waiting.

"Clocking in" everyday at a job they hated.

Almost letting fear stop them from walking away from their dead-end job forever.

But because of the Replens testing methods we teach, they realized there was nothing to be afraid of to begin with.

Click the link below to discover the exact, proven step-by-step process we use to replace our 9-5 job and build a life of freedom and abundance:

https://ko296.isrefer.com/go/ssmb/MMarkuson/

As you explore Amazon Replens on the next page, I hope it stirs something powerful in you about what is possible.

Thanks and God Bless..

Mike

www.ingramcontent.com/pod-product-compliance
Lightning Source LLC
Chambersburg PA
CBHW050821250726
48653CB00006B/2342